HERE'S HEATHCLIFF by Geo Gately

AMERICA'S CRAZIEST CAT!

Volume IV

THE BEST OF SUNDAY WITH HEATHCLIFF

HEATHCLIFF

AT HOME

A TOM DOHERTY ASSOCIATES BOOK

HEATHCLIFF AT HOME

Copyright © 1977, 1978, 1981 by McNaught Syndicate, Inc.

Reprinted by arrangement with Windmill Books, Inc. and Simon and Schuster, a division of Gulf and Western Corp.

First Tor printing: November 1985

A TOR Book

Published by Tom Doherty Associates, Inc.
49 West 24 Street
New York, N.Y. 10010

ISBN: 0-812-56810-9
CAN. ED.: 0-812-56811-7

Printed in the United States of America

0   9   8   7   6   5   4

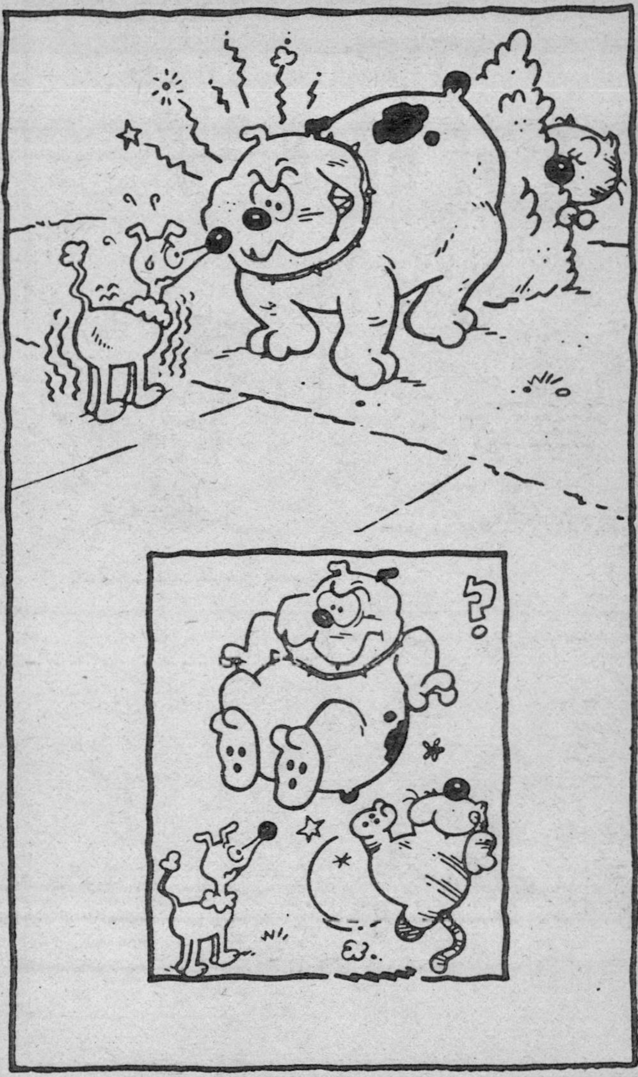

WE'LL NEVER GET ANY SLEEP!
HEATHCLIFF'S BACK FENCE SINGING IS GETTING OUT OF HAND!

THERE GOES THE BUNNY!
7
3
BUT WHAT'S THIS?! THERE'S A CAT ON THE TRACK!!
HE TAKES THE LEAD... HE'S FINISHING STRONG... HE WINS!
7

A STYLE
ALL HIS OWN

by
Gately

PRIZE CATCH!

by Bob Gately

PLUCK

OH, WOW! YOU'VE CAPTURED THE MEANEST GUY IN THE NEIGHBORHOOD!

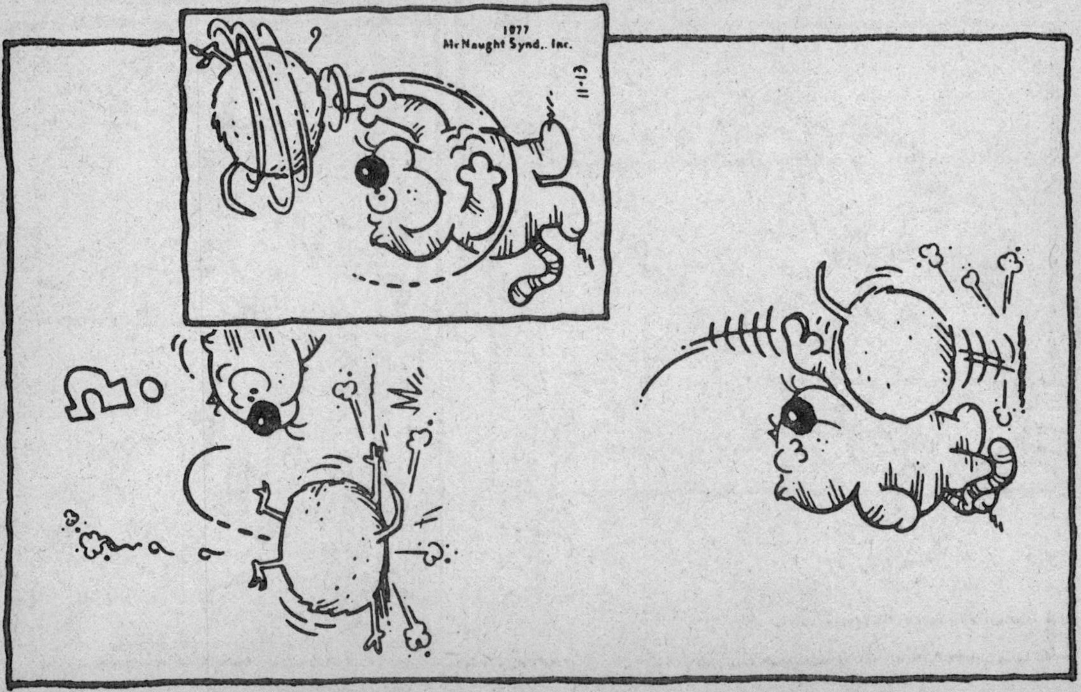
?
1977
McNaught Synd., Inc.
11-13

HE BREAKS ANOTHER TACKLE!...
HE'S AT THE TEN!...THE FIVE!....
HE GOES IN FOR THE T.D.!!!

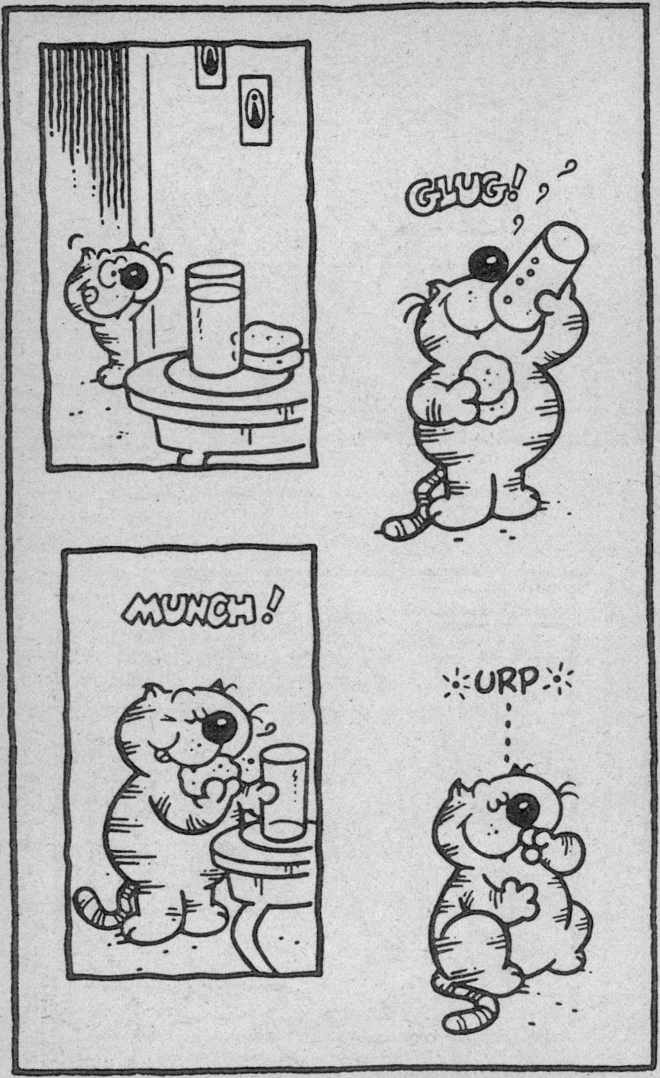
GLUG!
MUNCH!
URP

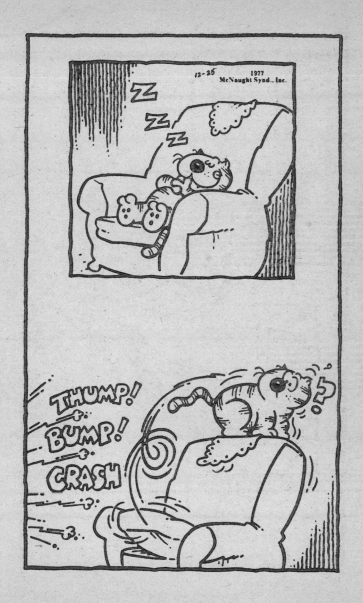

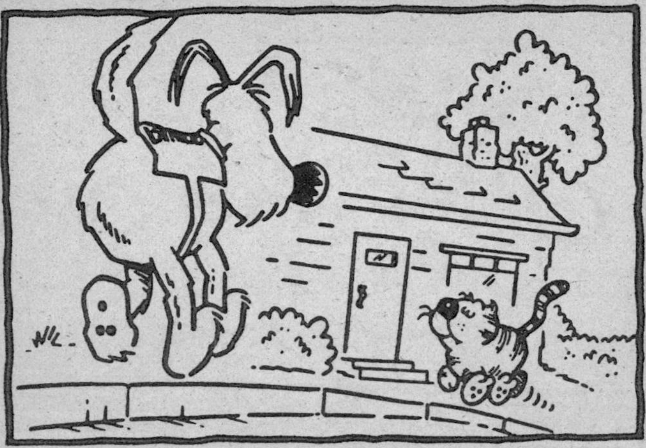

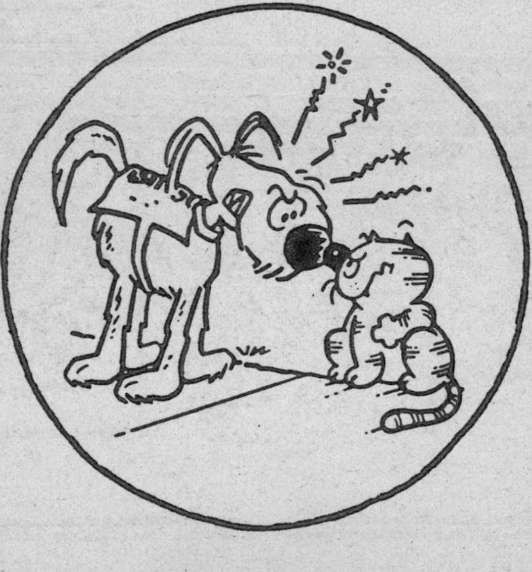

HEATHCLIFF

AMERICA'S CRAZIEST CAT

☐ 56800-1 SPECIALTIES ON THE HOUSE $1.95
    56801-X   Canada $2.50

☐ 56802-8 HEATHCLIFF AT HOME $1.95
    56803-6   Canada $2.50

☐ 56804-4 HEATHCLIFF AND THE $1.95
    56805-2   GOOD LIFE   Canada $2.50

☐ 56806-0 HEATHCLIFF: ONE, TWO, THREE $1.95
    56807-9   AND YOU'RE OUT   Canada $2.50

Buy them at your local bookstore or use this handy coupon:
Clip and mail this page with your order

TOR BOOKS—Reader Service Dept.
49 W. 24 Street, 9th Floor, New York, NY 10010

Please send me the book(s) I have checked above. I am
enclosing $_____ (please add $1.00 to cover postage
and handling). Send check or money order only—
no cash or C.O.D.'s.

Mr./Mrs./Miss _____

Address _____

City _____ State/Zip _____

Please allow six weeks for delivery. Prices subject to
change without notice.